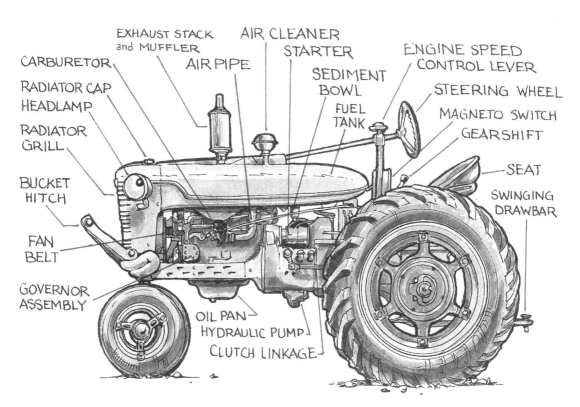

CARBURETOR

RADIATOR CAP
HEADLAMP

RADIATOR
GRILL

BUCKET
HITCH

FAN
BELT

GOVERNOR
ASSEMBLY

EXHAUST STACK
and MUFFLER
AIR PIPE

AIR CLEANER
STARTER

SEDIMENT
BOWL
FUEL
TANK

ENGINE SPEED
CONTROL LEVER

STEERING WHEEL

MAGNETO SWITCH
GEARSHIFT

SEAT

SWINGING
DRAWBAR

OIL PAN
HYDRAULIC PUMP
CLUTCH LINKAGE

Tractor Mac

This Is My Book

_____

To the Tenczas and
all 'tractor fixers', young and old,
who make tired iron run like new again.

Tractor Mac, LLC, Roxbury, CT 06783 USA
Visit www.tractormac.com

Tractor Mac
TUNE UP
Written and Illustrated by Billy Steers

To RUSSELL

2015

Billy Steers

Tractor Mac was always a smooth running, healthy tractor. The even sound of his engine could be heard in the fields from dawn till dusk.

"Chugga, chugga, chugga."
He never missed a day of work
at Stony Meadow Farm.

One day while pulling a heavy load,
Tractor Mac felt a pain and a pang.
He heard a *ping* and BANG!
"Chunka-klunk,
  chunka-clank,
    chunka-chunk."

"That doesn't sound so good,"
exclaimed Farmer Bill.
"It doesn't feel so good,"
thought Tractor Mac.

"That sounds like more
than I can fix out here,"
said Farmer Bill climbing
down from the big red
tractor. "I'd better call
Lou, the Tractor Doctor"

Dr. Lou stopped
by that afternoon.
"I've never felt like this
before," Mac told his
friend Sibley the workhorse.

"Hmmm," said Dr. Lou as he listened to Tractor Mac
and checked his engine.

"This is serious, Farmer Bill," said Dr. Lou. "It could be worn
bearings or a bent connecting rod. You should bring
Tractor Mac to my shop tomorrow."

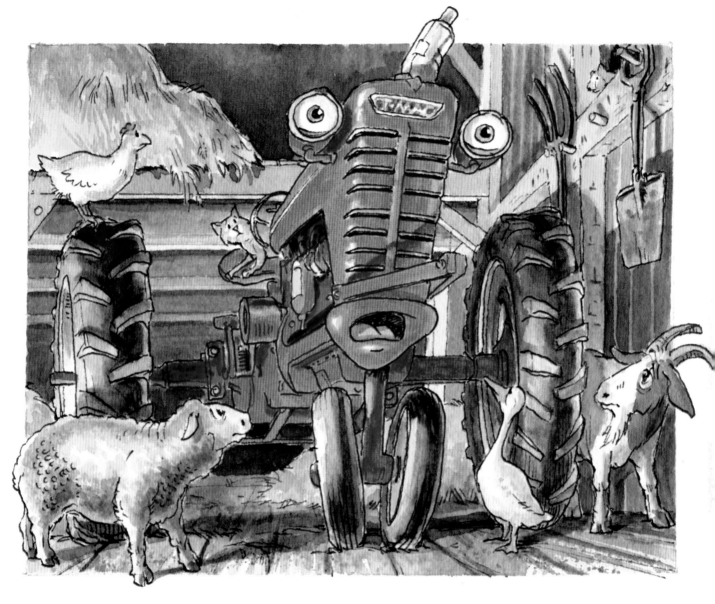

"I don't want to go to the hospital," groaned
Tractor Mac to his friends that evening.
"What if I can't be fixed? What if they sell me for parts?
Why does this have to happen to me?"

"Don't worry Tractor Mac, you'll be okay,"
mooed Margot the cow.
"We want to see you get better,"
clucked Carla the chicken.
"I'll give you my lucky horseshoe," said Sibley.

"You can have my four leaf clover for good luck,"
said Sam the ram.

The next day Farmer Bill brought Tractor Mac to
Dr. Lou's Tractor Clinic. "You'll be back to work soon,"
said Farmer Bill.

Tractors lined the yard of the clinic.
There were types of tractors Mac
had never seen before. "Bring him right in,"
Dr. Lou said to Farmer Bill.

ou've got nothing to
rry about," wheezed
iant tractor on
el wheels.

"Gus is always right," said a little riding mower.
"My name is Gasket. We've been here a long
time… but you're a *work* tractor!
You get to be fixed up first!"

Tractor Mac was wheeled into a clean workroom.

Dr. Lou and his helper, Steve, checked their tools and went straight to work.

Mac's oil was drained.

His hood removed.

The valve cover and cylinder head lifted off.

Then the pistons and rings were checked and repaired.

The sleeves and connecting rods
were checked…

and the engine block, oil pump,
and crankshaft inspected.

Replace, repair, and rebuild and re-grease!
Tractor Mac was then given a full tune up
with new spark plugs and wires.

"You sound much better, now!"
chuckled Gasket.
"It's back to work for you!" puffed Gus.
Tractor Mac smiled.
"I do feel much
better, thanks."

"He'll make a full recovery," beamed Dr. Lou.
"What a good patient he was."

Farmer Bill was happy to hear Mac's
smooth "chugga, chugga, chugga" again.

Tractor Mac was soon back at work.
"That's a healthy tractor!" cackled Carla.
"A real trooper" said Sam the ram.

"I love the sound of a
well tuned tractor,"
mooed Margot.

Late that summer Tractor Mac saw
Gus and Gasket at a farm show.
"Dr. Lou fixed you," said Mac.
"You're just like new!"

"I'm better than new!" exclaimed
Gasket. "I'm fit as a fiddle in my
working clothes!" said Gus.
"Hooray for tractor fixers!"
cheered Tractor Mac.

When
Giants
Roamed
the Earth
Make: International
Mode: Titan
Year: 1909

Billy Steers is an author, illustrator, and pilot. In addition to the Tractor Mac series, he has worked on forty other children's books. Mr. Steers had horses and sheep on the farm where he grew up in Roxbury, Connecticut. Married with three sons, he still lives in Roxbury.

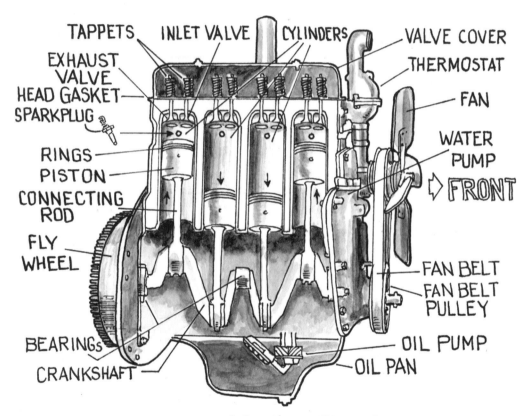

TAPPETS INLET VALVE CYLINDERS VALVE COVER

EXHAUST
VALVE THERMOSTAT

HEAD GASKET FAN

SPARKPLUG WATER
PUMP

RINGS FRONT

PISTON

CONNECTING
ROD

FLY
WHEEL FAN BELT

FAN BELT
PULLEY

BEARINGs OIL PUMP

OIL PAN

CRANKSHAFT

Tractor Mac's Engine